Set It & Don't Forget It
A Simple Guide to Investing

Joseph M. Romas

Paramount Publishing Company
Austin, Texas

Copyright © 2015 by Joseph M. Romas.
All rights reserved.

Published by
Paramount Publishing Company
Austin, TX 78734

ISBN: 978-0-692-38548-7
LCCN: 2 0 1 5 9 0 2 7 2 5

Cover designed by Stefanie McBride, http://www.stefaniemcbride.com
Cover photography by Erin Romas, http://www.vintagepeachphoto.com
Interior design by Danielle Acee, http://www.authorsassistant.com

Printed in the United States of America.

This book is dedicated to those
"who desire to live deep and suck out all the marrow of life."
(Henry David Thoreau)

QUOTES BY JOE ROMAS

"It's not what you know or even who you know, but rather the depth to which you know about who you know."

"I'd rather work eyes open to eyes shut for myself, than 8-12 hours for someone else."

"The more I learn about myself, the better and more successful I become."

"Be Heard, Not Herded."

Table of Contents

Who Should Read this Book?	i
Financial Disclaimer	ii
Preface	iii
What This Book Does	vi
The 3-Second Read	1
The 3-Minute Read	3
The 3-Hour Read	9
Investment Accounts	23
Retirement	27
Saving for Your Child's Education	29
Joe's Action Steps	31
Recommended Resources	37
Acknowledgments	38
Bibliography	40
About the Author	41

Who Should Read This Book

The information contained in this book is useful for, but not limited to:

- beginning investors;
- beginning financial advisors— especially those who have a nontraditional, academic financial background;
- assistants to financial advisors;
- experienced financial advisors who wish to provide valuable information to their clients in a clear, concise format;
- financial advisors whose clients would benefit from clear, concise advice in plain English;
- high school or college students who are new to the world of investing;
- teachers who teach and discuss money and/or investing with students.

Financial Disclosure

The material in this book is provided on a strictly informational and educational basis. This material is not to be taken as financial advice or as financial recommendations. Neither the author, nor the author's employers (past, present, and future), nor the publisher, shall be held liable or found negligent for any information in this book that is used and found unsuccessful. Stock investing involves risk, including the loss of principle. There is no guarantee that a diversified portfolio will enhance overall returns or outperform a non-diversified portfolio. Diversification does not protect against market risk. Withdrawals from a Roth IRA may be tax free, as long as they are considered qualified. Limitations and restrictions may apply. Withdrawals from a Traditional IRA prior to age 59 ½ may result in a 10% IRS penalty tax. Future tax laws can change at any time and may impact the benefits of Roth IRAs. Their tax treatment may change.

The author, author's employers, and/or publisher cannot be held liable for the information provided in this book. All ideas, concepts, and words are the author's intellectual property and belong to no one else. No legal action may be taken against the author nor anyone else involved in the publishing of this book for the information herein. Past performance of investments is no indication or prediction of future results.

PREFACE

My name is Joe Romas. In my time here on earth, I've held many roles, including United States Naval Officer and Student Naval Aviator; high school math and special education teacher; wealth planner; and now financial author. During my time as a wealth planner, I found it effective to explain concepts in groupings of three, which lead to the theme of three tied throughout this book.

Regarding my education and credibility in finance, I've passed the Series 7 General Securities Representative Exam, the Series 66 Uniform Combined Registered Investment Advisor exam, and the Wisconsin and Texas life and health insurance exams. Additionally, I chose to educate myself beyond what is required of financial advisors by obtaining a professional designation called the Accredited Asset Management Specialist or AAMS®. This designation was earned from the College for Financial Planning, and includes extensive study in the fields of asset management, risk/return and investment performance, taxation, investment strategies, retirement, insurance products, asset allocation and selection, estate planning, and regulatory and ethical issues for the investment professional. To find out more, you may "Google it."

Now that my credentials are listed, let's get to the good stuff. As a wealth planner, I LOVE working with people on their financial goals, visiting with them, and learning more about their past, present, and future. As a former teacher, one of my gifts is the ability to take complex topics and translate them into teachable, easily grasped concepts. I promise to do the same here. As Albert Einstein said, "Everything should be made as simple as possible, but no simpler."

While my work has been fulfilling and enjoyable, it does not define me as a person and I try not to take my jobs or myself too seriously. As my business mentor told me the other day, "We are all spiritual beings, just transitioning through the physical universe here we call earth." Therefore, I also define myself as a husband, a dad, a dog owner (through marriage), a son, a brother, a friend, and many more titles of this deeper nature.

This book is ultimately written with YOU in mind. It is not intended to badmouth anyone or fulfill any kind of personal agenda. My intent is that *you*, the person holding this book (iPad, iPhone, Kindle, Nook, or other device), will walk away with information that is valuable and practical.

Think of yourself as my friend, client, and partner in planning.

Moreover, if you will remember this simple concept, "**Set It and Don't Forget It**," you will have more financial confidence over the course of your life and be well on your way to LONG-TERM financial success, as YOU define it!

If you are struggling with money issues and need to find solace before investing, I recommend attending David Ramsey's **Financial Peace University** (FPU) *at least* once. Visit http://www.daveramsey.com to register for a class near you. I suggest taking the course in person to connect with other folks in similar situations. My wife Erin has taken the course twice, and I have taken FPU three times, along with Ramsey's business leadership course **EntreLeadership** once. I recommend the FPU course to those who are financially sound, as well as those who are financially "sick" (i.e. sick of their money worries). Dave Ramsey and his team share pearls of wisdom for everyone along the spectrum of financial understanding.

For as long as I have been an investor—about ten years now—I've learned that it is more important to simply DO SOMETHING rather than sit and do NOTHING. The investments you choose (known as your *investment selection*) and WHEN you choose to make them (also known as *market timing*) is less important to your long-term financial health than simply getting started. Reading this book is a great start toward making smart decisions about your money. Congratulations! Way to be proactive about your financial future!

By learning about *systematic investing* or *dollar-cost averaging*, as they say in my world, you will learn to harness the power of amazing concepts like *compound interest* and the *time value of money*. If this jargon intimidates you, *do not fear*. Through visuals and straight, simple language, I'll unlock the secret world of finances, so you can think about and discuss them easily, and then make sound decisions for yourself.

Lastly, this book contains information collected from numerous books on investing, finance, and personal finance. As a passionate investor and a dedicated wealth planner, my goal is to simply compile and highlight what I have learned over the last ten years and share it with you. This book is short, sweet, and to the point. I'm confident you'll find value here. Let's get started!

— Joe Romas

*Joe Romas is a registered representative with, and offers securities through, LPL Financial, Member FINRA/SIPC

What this Book Does

In this book I have compiled knowledge acquired over years of personal study, investing, and years in the financial services industry. I have removed the confusing verbage, fluff, and assembled it all into one, convenient place for you. I also take complicated topics like *Dollar-Cost Averaging*, *Asset Allocation*, and *Inflation*, which I call the "Greek and Latin of the industry," and translate them into plain English for you, my new friend and reader.

In the world of investing, it is very common for folks to get confused as to where to start. One of my mentors once said, "People in this business/industry often get paralysis by analysis." For example, if you think about all the possible types of investments, all the different companies that offer them, and all the different personalities of advisors, the task of investing proves daunting!

"Where do I start?"
"Where do I go?"
"Whom do I trust?"

The crucial and short answer to this long list of questions is, Just START INVESTING SOMETHING today and strongly consider investing in stocks/equities/companies of America and the world.

I remember another mentor imparting these words: "The best time to have planted a tree was twenty years ago; the second best time to plant a tree is today."

Today you'll start planting seeds of financial wisdom. How you choose to absorb this information is up to you.

- If you, like one of my family members, desire to finish this book in 3 seconds, go for it! You'll get the main point.

- If you choose to read like some of my clients, the book can be completed in 3 minutes. You'll get the main idea.

- If you are like most of my clients, and you're ready to *read it and take action*, it should take you about 3 hours. You'll not only grasp the beginning concepts of investing, you'll even take your first action steps.

Author and speaker Malcolm Gladwell said in his book *Outliers*, "In order for one to become a Phenom [successful in a field], he or she must put in 10,000 hours of time into a subject." I figure working about 55 hours per week and 50 weeks a year, I am right at the point of reaching 10,000 hours of assisting clients with their precious financial goals.

After four years of helping folks determine and pursue their financial goals, I find it almost selfish not to sit down and help others navigate the same immense learning curve I experienced in my early years of advising. I hope you'll take advantage of this offer and spend the full three hours to consume *and apply* this information.

My intention is to provide you with the education you will need to remain calm with your investments—like I had to remain calm from 2005 to 2011. If you remember, the years between 2007 and 2009 were tough! We experienced a global recession and global financial crisis. This means that there was a period of global economic/money slowdown, which contributed to many folks losing 35 to 50 percent of their 401(k), IRA, and other retirement account values in a relatively short period of time! It was a scary time for many families, but we can learn from this financial havoc and pursue our future financial goals with investments that are set appropriately.

I consider it my mission to educate you and free up your time to go out and "walk the dog." "Walk the dog" is code speak for STOP excessively looking at your investments, and do what it is you love to do when you are not at work!

Set it and don't forget it!

That is the beauty of this book. One of my intentions is to bring families back together (as if we all don't work enough hours in the week already, right?) and allow for things like eating dinner together, doing homework together, taking turns bathing the children, and so on. Who has the time to sit down and manage their investments with a fine-toothed comb these days?

With the method of investing I relay to you, I cannot guarantee your investments will outperform your neighbor, friend, or relative. I tell my clients what I'll tell you now; that my license does not allow me to *guarantee* them *anything*. If I did, I would lose my job. What I can guarantee, however, is that if you follow this advice, you will have more financial confidence than a VERY LARGE portion of your friends, family, neighbors, or golfing buddies who are subscribing to the next latest and greatest hot stock tip.

The perfect time to take action was YESTERDAY. Okay, maybe not yesterday, which, of course, is not possible, but I would encourage you to start something TODAY.

Time is ticking away, even as you and I share these ideas together. Nothing helps you gauge the passage of time better than watching your kids grow. Just ask my wife. Our daughter just turned two years old. It feels like just yesterday that we were taking her out into the frigid Wisconsin elements (we now reside in Austin, Texas as a result) from the hospital to our humble abode in Milwaukee!

With the ever-ticking clock in mind (visual on the cover for you), let me help get you started. Whatever time you have left on your side, let's take a step in the right direction to accumulate wealth. Wealth accumulation does not happen overnight, but rather over years of concentrated focus and effort. Although the concept is relatively simple, building, growing, keeping, and protecting wealth is not simple by any means.

I encourage you to get comfortable, grab a cup of your favorite warm or cold drink, temperature and geographic location depending, and imagine a close friend imparting wisdom and guidance in understandable words.

The 3-Second Read

Set it and don't forget it!

(It's that simple.)

THE 3-MINUTE READ

*It's not WHAT you invest in or
WHEN you chose to invest in it,
it's THAT you invest and
THAT you use asset allocation.*
—Determination of Portfolio Performance
by Brinson, Hood, and Beebower, 1986

Let's start with some definitions:

- **Stock**—Part ownership of a company. When you buy stock, you become a ***shareholder***.

- **Bond**—A loan to someone or an entity, which in turn puts your money to work and pays you interest for the use of your money.

- **Cash**—The money in your wallet, purse, under the mattress at home, or in the bank.

- **Portfolio**—All your investments considered together, even if they are at different financial outfits.

- **Assets**—A fancy term for items you own.

- **Asset Allocation**—Asset allocation is the amount or portion of money you have in stocks/equities, bonds, and cash. For example, you may choose to have 70% of your money (or assets) in stocks, 20% of your money in bonds, and 10% of your money in cash.

A portfolio that has all of its money in stocks is thought to have more risk associated with it than savings accounts or bonds, but stocks also have the potential to earn **more money long-term,** historically speaking.

A portfolio that has all of its money in bonds is thought to be safer or more conservative than an all-stock portfolio.

Some folks think that a safe way to keep money is in cash underneath the mattress or in cereal boxes, like the folks who lived through the Great Depression in the 1930s had a tendency to do. Jeremy Siegel, author of *Stocks for the Long Term,* illustrates this large mistake in his book. He talks about the return of cash being -1.4% annually, gold .7%, Bills (Treasury Bills) 2.7%, bonds 3.6% and stocks 6.6% real return (after inflation taken into account). These average returns are calculated from 1802-2012. All of this information begs the question, "Which of these investments/asset classes would you like to be invested in long-term?" Additionally, these are the returns after inflation, but think about the affect taxes would have on them as well! Remember, "It's not what you make that counts, it's what you keep."

The real risk investors face by holding cash in their portfolios is that cash/money loses about 3% of its purchasing power per year. This means that what you paid $1 for today, like a quart of milk, will, on average, cost $1.03 in one year and greater than $1.06 in two years (due to 3% interest instead of simple interest which would be exactly $1.06). In other words, you have to trade more money/dollars in exchange for that SAME quart of milk. Keep in mind, the size, quality, taste, and other similar features did not change at all.

It has been my experience that investors want to chase after and become entertained with picking the hottest investment fad and also trying to *time the market*.

TIMING THE MARKET

This is an attempt to purchase stocks before the market goes in the upward direction, OR, an attempt to sell stocks before the market goes in the downward direction. As my former freshman basketball coach would say, "This is fool's gold." Even Warren Buffet, one of the greatest stock investors of all time, has said that it is not possible to predict market movements, no matter what method you use to attempt to do so. There are just too many variables involved and too many geopolitical events that are liable to happen in such a short period of time (Russia/Crimea, 9-11-2001, Israel v. Palestine, etc.)

The Brinson Study [*Determination of Portfolio Performance* by Brinson, Hood, and Beebower, 1986], determined that asset allocation determined 94% of a portfolio's performance. ONLY 6% was attributed to other factors: market timing (4%) and investment selection (the remaining 2%).

What you need to know:

- A. Invest in a diversified portfolio made up of stocks and bonds, and think in terms of the companies you own instead of the companies that make up the stock market.

- B. A good "rule of thumb" is to use your age to determine asset allocation regarding stocks and bonds. 120 minus your age = % of allocation to put in stocks.

Here's an example to back up the theory. Let's say you are 30 years old.

$$120 - 30 = 90$$

The recommended percentage of stocks in your portfolio would therefore be 90% and your percentage of bonds would be 10%.

$$90\% \text{ stock} + 10\% \text{ bonds} = 100\% \text{ of your portfolio}$$

    C. Be patient, be disciplined, have faith, rebalance, diversify, and allocate your assets!

To maintain the appropriate ratio of stocks and bonds, consider **rebalancing** your portfolio on an annual basis, whether you do this on your own or with your financial advisor. This will maintain the appropriate amount of risk in your portfolio that you desire. Also, keep in mind that there is no guarantee that a diversified portfolio will enhance overall returns or outperform a non-diversified portfolio. Nonetheless, this rule of thumb will help with your overall efforts.

RISK

This is the amount of potential LOSS or GAIN you could see with your investments/money. Many investors and past clients have said they are tolerant (read *alright accepting*) of a lot of risk. In reality, they're lying to themselves and others. In an ideal world, we would all have 100% of our money in stocks and 0% in bonds (and cash) in our investment portfolios in order to maximize our long-term returns. However, this would inevitably lead to folks pulling their money out of their investments (from a behavioral perspective) if we have another year like 2008, which was a VERY BAD year for stocks overall.

A real-life example of managing your risk would be to pretend you have a portfolio (based on age, or 120 minus 40 = 80 for a 40-year-old person) of 80% stocks and 20% bonds. Now, if the STOCK market performs very well for a period of time and let's say the BOND market did very poorly, your portfolio might move into imbalance, with 95% of your money in stocks and 5% of your portfolio in bonds. You, you and your financial advisor, or your advisory team, would need to **re-allocate**, or **rebalance**, 15% of your money back into bonds from stocks. That would put you back at an 80:20 stock to bond balance, right where you desire to be based on your age and risk tolerance.

In the investing world I have learned and experienced that it is hard to come up with general rules of thumb. Nonetheless, some fairly common relationships exist and one can make some safe assumptions about them. Generally speaking, stocks and bonds tend to move in opposite directions. Therefore, if the bond market makes a comeback, as it historically does, since markets tend to move in cycles, you will have 20% of your money as opposed to 5% of it in bonds, and this would be better for your performance, but more importantly, for RISK EXPOSURE in the long run.

How the money gets rebalanced is a function of who handles your investments. You can rebalance the account yourself if you are a Do-It-Yourselfer. You and your financial advisor can rebalance your portfolio. Or your advisory team can rebalance your portfolio automatically for you for a certain percentage of your assets per year if you prefer to take a more hands-off approach to investing. Typically this fee-based program will run you anywhere from 1.0% to 2.5% per year of the overall amount in your fee-based account.

For example, if you have $50,000 in your advisory account, and pay 2% per year, you will pay $1,000 per year in expenses/value to your financial services firm. Watch out for additional expenses in these programs, added by the "Annual Operating Expenses" of the investments used in these accounts. This is a normal expense, but make sure you know what it is. For example, you may pay 1.5% to your financial services firm, and also pay an additional 1% in average operating expenses in the investments they choose for you to invest in. This adds up: 1.5% + 1% = 2.5% of your money in total expenses.

Set It and Don't Forget It!
(End of 3-minute read)

THE 3-HOUR READ

Working with a Financial Advisor versus Do It Yourself (DIY)

DO IT YOURSELF VERSUS WORKING WITH AN ADVISOR
If you are absolutely convinced you must be a do-it-yourself investor, and are ABSOLUTELY POSITIVE you will not make "The BIG Mistake"—which would be to pull all of your money out of stocks when the market is low—look up Vanguard, T. Rowe Price, Fidelity, or another simliar company. Just beware that you may have to call an 800-number and press 1 for English, instead of getting through to a person, as you would if you were to work with one of the companies mentioned below.

You can always buy investments online; however, you are not able to buy a financial plan online. This is why I recommend working with a comprehensive advisor regarding planning. Financial advisors, if they're worth anything, will consider taxation and estate planning when recommending investments and vehicles for wealth accumulation and preservation.

If you want an advisor who is there to help you through the good times and the bad, and assist you in controlling your behavior and emotions, you may want to visit with an advisor at Merrill Lynch, LPL (**Linsco Private Ledger** – for independent financial advisors), UBS, New York Life, or another similar company. You may pay more in expenses than you would with Fidelity or Vanguard, but it will probably be worth it and prove VALUABLE to you if you enjoy a more personalized approach to planning. In my opinion, this is the area that the large majority of investors and the general population, need to participate in.

Remember, their time is valuable—like yours. Before you sit down with an advisor, prepare a list of questions ahead of time to keep the conversation efficient, and make sure you get all the necessary information you require. Most advisors will offer a free consultation to see if it makes sense mutually to begin an advisor/client relationship.

Note on working with an advisor: In my opinion, only about 1% of the population should truly be Do-It-Yourselfer investors, because 99% of folks do not have adequate time, focus, or most important, knowledge of this subject. To reiterate an important point, I recommend working with a financial advisor unless you absolutely know you will never make The Big Mistake.

The Big Mistake is pulling your investments out of the market at the very bottom of a stock market downturn—a.k.a. the "Bear Market". Currently, as of 1/05/2015, from the bottom of the S&P 500 in March of 2009, we have experienced a 199.22% increase/recovery!

The stock market has a positive bias attached to it. In plain English, this means that the market tends to go up, down, and sideways over the short-term, but over the long-term historically speaking, the market trends in an upward direction.

Convince yourself of this. Do a Google search and print out any 80-year return of the S&P 500, then draw a line through all the peaks and valleys of the graph. I can assure that your line will be going in the upward direction from left to right over the course of time.

In addition, the 1979, Kahneman and Tversky prospect theory cluded that the pain of a loss is much stronger and more pow_____ than the positive emotions felt from a gain. In other words, no one likes to lose his or her hard-earned dollars. The good news: you do not lose your hard-earned dollars if you do not sell when your emotions are telling you to sell. This is called *paper loss*, and it will happen to an investor many times over his or her investing life. The bold number on your statement simply cannot continue to always go up monthly, quarterly, or annually, when you are in the habit of investing. So, just set it and try to forget it– at least for a while!

ABOUT INFLATION

Inflation is the term we give to the fact that items we purchase on a daily basis get more expensive at the rate of about 3% every year. Remember the milk example I gave earlier? This could decrease and become 1% every year, or it could increase and become 4% every year. We just do not know. It is hard to tell, but historically, it seems as though 3 to 4% should be adequate for planning purposes. The tricky thing about inflation is you cannot see it, hear it, taste it, smell, it, or touch it. It is the silent thief of your very hard-earned dollars.

If your investment is not averaging more than 3% every year, you are safely losing money (1% minus 3% = -2%) or treading water (3% - 3% = 0%).

If you hold your money in cash, you now have a real return of (0% - 3% = -3%). Again, safely losing money.

Only when you get above 3% are you able to realize a *net gain* (4% - 3% = 1%).

ABOUT TAXES

Caution: Do not forget about taxation. It is not what you make necessarily, it is what you keep. If you have a (7% - 3% = 4%) gain, your gain will only be 3% if you are in a 25% income effective tax situation. This is because 25% of your 4% return goes to the IRS. Make sense? Here is the math, for those of you math nerds out there like myself. (.25 x 4(%) = 1(%)) So, 1% of your return will go to the IRS for tax purposes. Therefore, 4% - 1% = 3% real return.

Also, do not WORRY about paying taxes. I educate my clients that, as their financial advisor, the largest financial problem I want them to have is the problem of paying too much in taxes. Paying taxes means that they have money, and their jobs and existing money are making money for them.

Nevertheless, make sure you have discussions with your professionals (accountant, tax-preparer, CPA) about being tax-conscious and tax-efficient.

TOO MUCH TRADING CAN COST YOU

Another valid reason to work with an advisor is to prevent you from trading too much. One of my mentors stated it perfectly and taught me, "Sometimes a portfolio is like a wet bar of soap—the more you play around with it, the smaller it gets."

Transaction fees, commissions, and fees for trading are all ways to see your portfolio dwindle if too much trading is done too often. I am not instructing you to let bad investments continue; I am telling you to follow a more ***buy-and-hold quality investments*** approach, rather than becoming a day trader on your own or with a broker/financial advisor.

In his book, *Behavioral Investment Counseling*, Nick Murray says that those who work with an advisor and think long-term have a much better chance of a higher long-term return and are much more likely not to derail themselves from their own financial goals.

Please, be careful and educate yourself if you are thinking of investing on your own. You may be your own worst enemy when you are investing. Benjamin Graham said it best: "The investor's chief problem—and even his worst enemy—is likely to be himself."

On the flip side, if you have adequate knowledge of investing, diversifying, and KNOW that you will continue to let your investments "ride on" in the case of a market downturn, you have my rare blessing to be a "Do-It-Yourselfer." You would be among the few and far between in the investing population.

One of the savviest investors ever and a student of investor behavior, Sir John Templeton, said, "Bull markets are born on pessimism, grow on skepticism, mature on optimism, and die on euphoria."

- **Bull market**—When the market is traveling in the upward direction ("good")

- **Bear market**—When the market is heading in the downward direction ("bad")

Long-term focus investors like bull markets!

DCA

Goal: Efficiently investing money each month over a long period of time.
Position Bias: Over time the market tends to rise so your shares will have greater value.

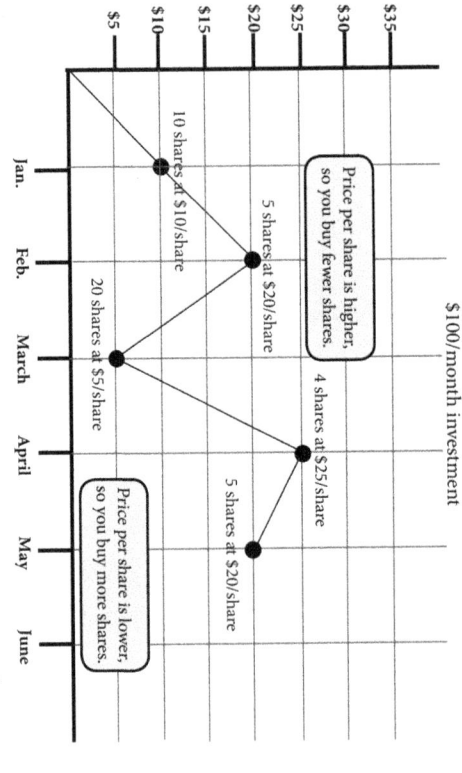

Over a 5-month period, you have invested $500. You have purchased 10 + 5 + 20 + 4 + 5 = 44 shares. These shares are valued at $20/share, which means your investment is worth 44 x $20/share = $880.00. This does not take into account dividend reinvestment and may help even out market dips and rises.

This is a hypothetical example and is not representative of any specific investment. Stock investing involves risk, including the loss of principle.

Dollar Cost Averaging

When you **Set It and Don't Forget It**, you are efficiently investing your money. Again, I believe it is more important THAT you invest your money, than WHAT you invest those hard-earned dollars in.

Let's use an investment of $100/month as an example. In plain English, when the market is up—meaning we are experiencing a bull market—or "expensive," as I like to say to my clients, your $100/month will buy you fewer shares of an investment

When the market is a "bear" market, or "inexpensive," as I like to call it, you will be using your $100 to buy more shares at a lower price. Don't worry about how much—just to do something within your means, even if it is $15/month.

If you are a higher income earner and are able to put away the maximum annual amounts, which change yearly, do so. For example, in 2014, you could put as much as $17,500 a year ($1,458.33/month, which does not include your employer's match) into your 401k and $5,500 a year ($458.33/month) into your Roth IRA. This can change slightly from year to year. Your CPA or tax preparer will know the current limits.

Some folks will ask me, "Who determines the max annual contribution limits for the Roth, 401k, and other limiting plans?" The answer: the Internal Revenue Service. Well, technically it is Congress that creates and enacts the tax code; it is the IRS that enforces it.

COMPOUND INTEREST

- **Interest**—Money earned on the investment of your money (principal) into a stock, bond, Certificate of Deposit (CD), or other vehicle. More simply, it is the growth portion of your investment.

When a dollar is invested, there are two different ways it can earn interest. It can gain *simple interest* or it can earn *compound interest*.

Your money invested in stocks has the opportunity to earn interest in a *compound* form. This means that your money is not only earning interest on the principal, or the amount you contributed, but it also earns interest on the interest paid on your money over the years.

For example, let's say you invest $100 and no more ever again. If your investment averages a 10% return on an annual basis, after the first year you would have $110. The second year, keeping in mind an average annual return of 10%, you would have $121 (NOT $120, as that would be **simple interest**). This is because you earned interest on the principal the first year, which was $100. You earned interest on the principal ($100) plus interest ($10) the second year, so you start with $110, and 10% of $110 is $11.

So $110 + $11 = $121 after year two. Then in year three, you would end up with $133.10 because $121 + $12.10 = $133.10. Make sense? Now, let's say we got dedicated and started having $100 taken out of our checking account on a monthly basis. Also, I am going to assume the person is 33 years old (like myself) and plans to retire at age 63. If we assume a 9% rate of return on our investment, we would end up with $179,213 after only putting away $100/month! For the price of not going to a little place I like to call *FIVEbucks*, for a month, we can put that coffee money away, brew our coffee at home, and really make our money grow. In other words, a dollar today is way more valuable later on, but we must be patient with time to allow our money to have the potential to grow and compound. Albert Einstein, unarguably a man that discovered some powerful things said this of compound interest, "Compound interest is the most powerful force in the universe." Whether he *actually* said it or not, I would recommend choosing to adopt this as your new philosophy.

THE TIME VALUE OF MONEY & THE "COST" OF WAITING

This topic illustrates why it is important to start your investments TODAY and not "soon," "later," "when the bad news is over," or "when the market isn't quite so high." Insert your own reason here for why you may wait to invest. In real life, starting with the media there will always be plenty of reasons to wait and not invest. "If it bleeds, it leads" is certainly true. Turn your television news channel off, put the paper away, and go outside and play with your family. Additionally, you may choose to walk the dog.

In his Financial Peace University program, which should be a requirement to graduate from high school AND college, Dave Ramsey uses two different characters named Ben and Arthur as an example. Ben invests only $2,000/year from age 19 to age 26 (7 years) and after $16,000 of total dollars invested, he stops. Arthur invests $2,000/year from age 27 to age 65 (38 years), his retirement age.

Who ends up with more money? Arthur, right? Because he invested over $78,000 and Ben invested just $16,000 total dollars? WRONG! Arthur ends up with $1,532,166 and Ben ends up with $2,288,996! This is a difference of over $755,000. (Note: These numbers assume a 12% rate of return).

What is the only thing the two men did differently? Ben started when he was 19 and had TIME on his side! [Note: Past performance is no indicator or guarantee of future performance, so the rate of return could have been 4%, 7%, 16%, or something else].

If the annual average performance had been less than 12%, their final amounts would have been closer.

If the annual average performance had been more than 12%, there would have been an even bigger difference in their final totals. So, performance (percent return) does matter as well!

In addition to just simply beginning to save, the important point of the Ben and Arthur story is to get started as soon as humanly possible. Nick Murray, a financial advisor for over 45 years, says, "Remember that the long-term compound return of the S&P 500 of about ten percent, the last dollar a 45-year old spends is fifteen dollars his 75-year-old self will not have."

This is crucial to understand. Another example would be my prospective client John Doe, who walked out the other day and right away said, "I need one year to begin investing." I told him that was fine and that I was in no rush for him to begin, but that HE needed to be in a rush for him to begin.

To illustrate this point to him, I ran numbers for him on my future value calculator, which showed that by failing to invest $50 per month for the next 29 years instead of 30 (because he would miss the next 365 days of investing, his account would have been worth $56,676 instead of $52,407, "costing" him $4,268.

For the record and to appease the analytical folks out there, I assumed a 7% annual average rate of return. Had he started today and put in $50 per month (or $600 per year), he lost out on $4,268, which would have only cost him $600 now over the next year of investing. This is the power of compound interest in combination with the time value of money at its best!

WHY INVEST?

I am often asked, "Joe, why should I invest my money at all? Wouldn't it be better to put money into a CD, money market, savings account, under my mattress, or some other safe place?"

The answer is: your money would silently be eaten up by inflation. Inflation is the fancy term for the fact that things get more expensive as time goes on. I often show clients a 10-cent stamp from 1975, and then compare it with today's 49-cent stamp. A drastic increase in postage has occurred over the last 38 years. Not only has the price doubled from 10 cents to 20 cents, but also it has doubled AGAIN from 20 cents to 40 cents. It is not that the VALUE of the stamp has increased for you as a buyer of a stamp, right? That stamp still mails the same letter, takes the letter the same distance, through the same methods used in 1975. (Of course, I'm sure there is technology now to make it faster and more efficient. I would just have to call my father who has been a mail carrier for over 30 years now.) Nonetheless, mailing a letter today takes more of your pennies now, because the pennies are not worth as much as they used to be. For that matter, NEITHER are your dollars.

It is said that wealth flows from those not willing to take risks with their time and money to those willing to take risks with their money, time, and lives. This holds true especially in a capitalistic economy here in the United States. Additionally, the real risk you run by not investing your money is that someday you may outlive it by sticking it underneath the mattress or putting it in CDs that yield .1% interest. The term I have started using with my clients for return on a CD (Certificate of Deposit) is *point pitiful*.

Risk Tolerance

Some more definitions:

- **Risk Averse**—What most people label conservative. It is being overly protective of your principal and money, and in return, receiving a low return or low interest as a result.

- **Aggressive**—The opposite of conservative and what some call, risk tolerant. A portfolio of 100% stock and 0% bonds and cash is thought to be an example of an aggressive way one can invest money. Generally speaking, the greater the risk the greater the long-term return.

The following risk tolerance assessment links can be very helpful. Take a few minutes to choose one and complete. Many people initially feel they would fall in one category but in reality, they fall somewhere entirely different! Take one, quick!

Google "Risk Tolerance Questionnaire" and find one for yourself that you like that takes not only your tolerance for risk into consideration, but also your life stage or age.

Let's say that on a Risk Tolerance scale of 1 to 5, with 1 being the most risk averse and 5 being the most aggressive, where do you find yourself? If you find yourself in the 1 to 3 range, work with a financial advisor to talk you off the ledge when another significant downturn happens in the market. When I say *significant downturn*, I mean the 38% drop that happened between 2007 and 2009.

Simply consider my rule of thumb for asset allocation (ratio of stocks to bonds based on your age, as mentioned in ***The 3-Minute Read*** under ***Timing the Market***), and do not become so fixated on trying to fine-tune your asset allocation based on your risk tolerance considerations.

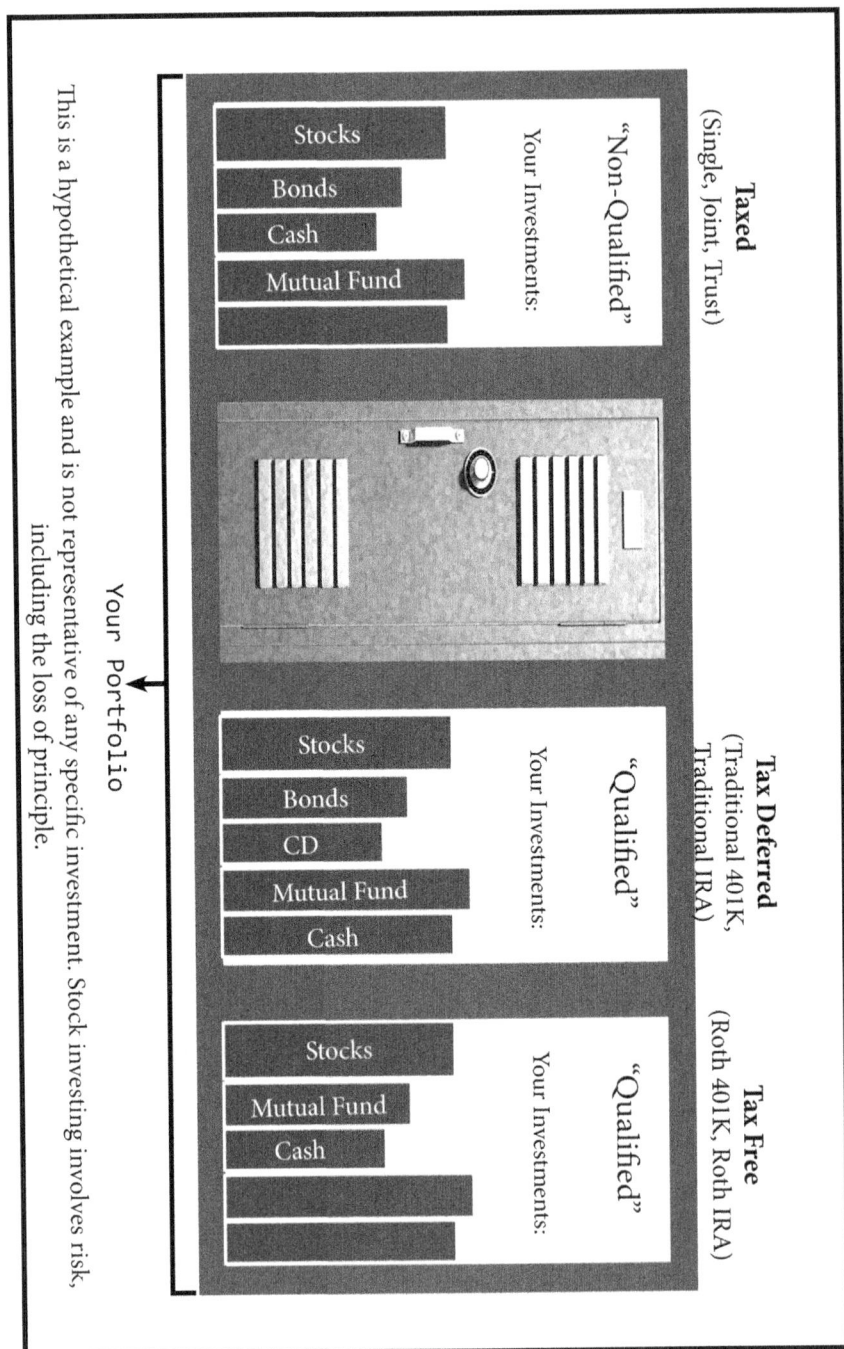

The Three Main Types of Investment Accounts

Continuing with my theme of three, the three main types of investment accounts you can open up are:

1. Taxed accounts
2. Tax-deferred accounts
3. Tax-free accounts

I like to think of investment vehicles (stocks, bonds, mutual funds, and so on) as books that go on shelves and account types as lockers—like the one you used to put your books in at high school. By the way, can you still remember whose locker was to your left and right? Back in your high school days, when you were learning about such important (*not!*) topics such as the Pythagorean Theorem, biological definitions, and sentence structure; instead of cooking, budgeting, investing, and practical things you might actually use on a daily basis?

Apologies. I'll get off my education soapbox now. I do realize there is a time and place for geometry and that folks such as engineers need to specialize in certain areas to contribute to society. Just know that I used to be a high school math teacher, so education is something that I am interested in and passionate about. Can you tell? Now, back to the topic at hand.

TAXED ACCOUNTS

A taxed account is taxed when you sell investments out of the account during that tax year, earn capital gains, or earn dividends in your investment vehicles. For example, if you own KO (Coca Cola) and sell it at a gain (the value of the stock is up compared to when you bought it) in 2013, you would pay taxes on the gains in 2013. Examples of taxed investment accounts would include:

- Individual accounts (or single accounts)
- Joint accounts
- Trust accounts

TAX-DEFERRED ACCOUNTS

A tax-deferred account is taxed in the future, when you pull the money out. Typically, for most of my clients, this happens in retirement when they are no longer working full-time. The money taken out of the tax-deferred account will be taxed at whatever your tax rate is in your future.

"What will my tax rate be in the future?" I am asked all too often. The answer is, "Your guess is as good as mine." I would say tax rates will likely be higher in the future than what they are today in 2015. Wouldn't you agree? Try telling your neighbor that taxes will be lower in the future, and let me know what they say. Examples of tax-deferred accounts include:

- Traditional 401(k)
- Traditional IRA (individual retirement account)
- SIMPLE (Savings Incentive Match Plan for Employees) IRAs
- SEP (Simplified Employee Pension) IRAs

TAX-FREE ACCOUNTS

A tax-free account is taxed now and the earnings are TAX FREE! Almost every person who reads this book should take full advantage of the fact that your money has the opportunity to grow, WHILE YOU DO NOTHING to make it grow… tax free! **My urgent recommendation: Get money into one of these accounts while this is still the case.** I am not saying I can predict the future, but you never know when this rule may change and you may be grandfathered in.

There are some rules as to when the earnings on the money are not tax-free, but as long as you do not touch the earnings until you are 59-1/2 years old and have had the Roth for five or more years, you can access the principal (the amount you invested/contributed) and the interest/earnings (the amount it gained) tax free. Examples of tax-free accounts include:

- Roth IRA (sometimes referred to as a "Roth")

- Roth 401k (some of you may have this at your work, and it is slowly becoming more popular).

WHICH KIND OF ACCOUNT IS BETTER?

I get the following popular question on a monthly basis, "Which is better to invest in, the tax-deferred account or the Roth account?" The answer: Consider both of them.

I tell folks, as outlined in my steps, to make sure to put away at least as much as your company's match in the 401(k), and then put the rest into a Roth IRA—unless your company has a Roth 401(k). Usually I answer your question with "It really depends on your age and your tax bracket."

As a rule of thumb, the best place to put money when you are young (20s, 30s, 40s, and even 50s) is the Roth.

If you are a high income earner and are not allowed by the IRS to contribute to a Roth account (ask your tax professional about this), or you have a tax issue, meaning you are in a high tax bracket, I recommend putting the money into a traditional 401k and a traditional IRA, instead of the Roth, for the $5,500 (2013 tax year) tax deduction. Just know that once you make over a certain amount of income, you are only allowed to deduct a portion or none of your contribution.

This topic is one that would be smart to consult with your CPA and financial advisor. Your financial advisor (if he or she is worth his or her weight) ought to have software that determines if it is appropriate to contribute to the Roth IRA or Traditional IRA. Also, he or she will be able to determine if a *Roth Conversion* might be appropriate for some or all of your Traditional IRA. A Roth Conversion gets a bit technical, and I'll leave it outside the scope of this book. If I determine the demand to be there, like there was for this book you hold, perhaps there can be another edition or another book in the future with more topics and more complex strategies. Now do you see why it pays to work with an advisor that sees things differently or ideas you may not know of or think of?

What type of account you choose is not a topic to lose sleep over, especially with an advisor on your side. Just contribute SOMETHING on a regular basis! Then **Set It and Don't Forget It!**

WHAT ABOUT RETIREMENT?

Your Job or Your Business's Retirement Plan Help (401k, 403b, 457, SEP (Simplified Employee Pension), etc.)

401K ALLOCATION HELP

I receive a lot of questions about how to allocate money in a 401k. By 401k, I mean anything your employer offers, which could be a 403b, 457, Simple IRA, SEP IRA, profit sharing, or other vehicle.

If you are not concerned about fees, consider a portfolio closest to the year you plan to retire. It is designed to diversify your investments automatically and not put all your eggs in one basket. This approach is engineered to gradually make you a more conservative investor as time goes on.

What I mean by conservative is that your asset allocation (aren't you glad you understand that now? You ought to be excited about learning the Greek and Latin of the financial industry!) will move you from a more-stock focus the younger you are, to a more bond-focused approach the older you get.

For example, if you plan to retire in 2033, consider a portfolio closest to this time frame/year and go out and "walk the dog." If you plan to retire in 2032, consider a portfolio closest to this time frame/year and go out and "walk the dog."

But BEWARE! These investments sometimes have high fees. This means that if you yield 7% average annual return, and the company managing the investments would earn 1.25% of your return, you would end up getting a net return of 5.75%. Talk with your financial professional about expenses and fees.

You may be asking, "So what do I do then?" And there are a few answers. You may consider:

- Talking to your 401k plan's financial advisor—if this person comes to your workplace and properly services you as a client.

- Talking to a financial advisor from Vanguard, LPL (Linsco/Private Ledger) who helps clients of independent financial advisors, TD Ameritrade, T. Rowe Price, Charles Schwab, Fidelity, and other financial services companies that can assist you with your financial goals. They are listed here in no particular order and some of them have their own investments as well.

- If you choose not to work with an advisor for whatever reason, look at the LONG-TERM returns (5 to 10-year returns), not SHORT-TERM returns (1 to 3-year returns) of the investments you are thinking of selecting. However, I would not recommend doing this. If you choose to go this direction, an easy rule of thumb is to pick the percentage of stock investments in your portfolio based on the formula (120 - your age). For example, if I were 33 years old, I would look at an 87% stock investment and 13% bond investment mix (or 90% stock and 10% bond mix if you wanted to round off).

529 Plans for Your Child's College Education

A 529 plan is a college savings plan named after Internal Revenue Code 529, which was created to help investors plan for higher education expenses. It is an individually designed, state-sponsored investment program that acts like a Roth IRA for qualified education expenses. The owner of the account is the adult, and the beneficiary will be the person attending college in the future.

As Phil Demuth says in his book, *The Affluent Investor*, do not worry about the impact of having a 529 for your child or grandchild's education on FAFSA (Free Application for Federal Student Aid) or scholarships. If you are motivated and disciplined to follow the teachings of this book to begin with, you more than likely will not qualify for much, if any, financial aid anyway.

While it is noble and admirable to want to save for your child's or grandchild's college, I advise my clients, especially parents, to think about their retirement first and THEN to fund the 529 plan for their loved ones. It's great if your son or daughter can attend Harvard fully funded by you, but it's not so great if you have to move back in with that child after he or she graduates from that prestigious school! Get the idea? It may sound selfish, but it's NOT!

I know that my daughter Sofia will be thankful her mom and dad won't be moving in with her later in life! My wife and I have collected birthday and Christmas money for Sofia in her 529 plan for college over the past several years. My little peanut already has way more money saved for college than I did at age 18!

A great resource for college saving and how to afford the rapidly rising costs of higher education can be found at http://www.savingforcollege.com.

* **Disclosure:** Prior to investing in any 529 plan, investors should consider whether the investor's or designated beneficiary's home state offers any state tax or other benefits that are only available for investments in such state's qualified tuition program. Withdrawals used for qualified expenses are federally tax free. Tax treatment at the state level may vary. Please consult with your tax advisor before investing. Tax laws are subject to change. Please discuss your specific situation with a qualified tax advisor.

Joe's Investment Action Steps

1. Have a Plan
2. Consider Life Insurance
3. Create and Build an Emergency Fund
4. Match Your Employer's Contribution to Your Plan
5. Consider a Roth IRA

Action Step 1: Have a Plan

Have a budget. Spend less than you make, and invest/save some of the rest. Make a list of where every dollar goes for a month. How can you begin to invest if you don't know what you have to invest with? EVERY dollar needs to be accounted for and put toward something, whether it is investing, mortgage, cell phone, food, date night, and so on.

Action Step 2: Consider Life Insurance

Make sure you have life insurance coverage BEFORE YOU INVEST A DOLLAR. This is, heaven forbid, just in case you do not wake up tomorrow. A mortifying thought, but it has happened before. Life insurance is NOT for you, and it is NOT an investment (in most cases). It is intended to provide money for your spouse, kids, or anyone else dependent on your income while you are alive. The money will help them replace your income/paycheck in the event that you do not wake up tomorrow.

If you follow the teachings of the book, you will not have a need for life insurance when you are older and your children are grown and independent. You will be self-insured at that point in your life.

Term versus Permanent (Universal Life, Variable Universal Life, Whole Life, etc) Insurance

A common question about life insurance I receive is about the differences in buying term or permanent life insurance. There are so many debates and so many different philosophies on this that if you asked 10 different people, you would get 10 different answers. What I teach folks is, like anything else, study your options carefully and ask many questions until you understand it for your situation. Ask:

- *Why do I need life insurance?*
  Answer: To replace your income if you pass away.

- *What do I want the life insurance to be for?*
  Answer: Typically, you want the life insurance to help out heirs who are not able to work, like your minor children. However, in some advanced planning stages, heirs can use life insurance payments to maximize tax efficiency, leverage money, and protect businesses from having to close their doors.

- *When do I want the life insurance to protect my family?*
  Answer: If you want protection from death now, term is usually the way to go. If you want protection from death at the end of your life expectancy, in your 70s, 80s, 90s, and not all that uncommon nowadays 100s, you will want to look at purchasing permanent or "whole life" insurance. Keep in mind that the cost of permanent life insurance ("premium") is much higher than term insurance, especially early on in the policy.

ACTION STEP 3: CREATE AND BUILD AN EMERGENCY FUND
Having an Emergency Fund brings peace of mind to everyone. An Emergency Fund is built up in case your car needs a repair or the furnace breaks down. Going out to dinner because you had a rough day does not warrant taking money from this emergency fund.

Most advisors encourage you to have three to six months of living expenses in a fully funded Emergency Fund. My family's Emergency Fund target is approximately $10,000, which we put into a ***money market*** account. (A money market account is like a savings account with the potential to earn more interest; however, there may be a limit on annual withdrawals). If you would like to attempt to earn more interest on your Emergency Fund, and are willing to take some risk, you can consider putting this money into a conservative investment.

ACTION STEP 4: MATCH YOUR EMPLOYER'S CONTRIBUTION TO YOUR PLAN
It is important to contribute up to the match (most companies match 3 to 6% of your salary) into your work's 401k/403b/457 plan. The earnings in this account are tax-deferred and will be taxed later when you pull it out at your tax rate (preferably, you will pull it out IN retirement, to take full advantage of the tax-deferred growth potential). Ideally, you will want to wait until 59-1/2 years old to withdraw these funds. There are exceptions, which are outside the scope of this book.

Side note: If you are in a low income tax bracket right now (10 to 25%), the ROTH IRA/401k is definitely where you want to consider putting your money in order to get taxes out of the way now.

If you are in a high tax bracket and are trying to get into a lower one, you will want to consider putting some or all your contributions into a Traditional 401k and/or Traditional IRA.

Action Step 5: Consider a Roth IRA

If you have contributed to your employer's retirement plan up to the match, then consider a Roth IRA for the rest of your investable dollars. Do not pass up all those years of potential tax-free growth and earnings! Also, this helps you get another "locker" of money established so that in retirement, you have two different buckets of money to pull from. Again, please consult your financial advisor and tax preparer on this topic.

WRAPPING **I**T **U**P

Needless to say, by no means has this been an *exhaustive* course about investing in three seconds, three minutes, or three hours, however you chose to read the book! Moreover, I am still on a path of mastering all I can about investing. I want to better myself and more importantly, help my clients and prospective clients achieve their financial goals.

One of my mentors once said, "In this business, you will never know everything. It's more about the journey than the destination."

This is a liberating feeling because you and I cannot possibly know all there is to know about the beast we call investing. I recommend educating yourself, finding a trusted financial advisor, and then trust that you are doing what is best given the knowledge you had to make your decisions. Allow yourself some grace if you find out information that you had not known earlier. For example, you may find thorough reading this book that you are paying extremely high fees for an account. Chalk it up to a great learning experience and simply move on. This is a waste of time and will drive you out of your mind if you dwell on anything but the present moment.

Much of my investing knowledge has come from trial and error with my own portfolio. In addition, I have worked with hundreds of clients and have seen the mistakes they or their previous advisors have made as well. This book compiles years of personal growth, knowledge, and lessons from the school of hard knocks telling you what to do, and what NOT to do!

What should you take from this read?

DON'T WAIT! Get out there and get something started today. Get rid of your fear, have faith in the future, and do not let paralysis by analysis get the best of you and your financial success!

I will leave you with a quote: "Faith by itself, if it is not accompanied by action, is dead."

I also maintain "Knowledge, if it is not accompanied by action, is dead." So, please do not just read this book…Go and take action NOW!

RECOMMENDED READINGS

The One Thing
by Gary Keller & Jay Papason

Secrets of the Millionaire Mind
By T. Harv Eker

Rich Dad Poor Dad
By Robert Kiyosaki

Dave Ramseys Financial Peace University
By Dave Ramsey

Think and Grow Rich
By Napoleon Hill

The Miracle Morning
By Hal Elrod

The Alchemist
By Paulo Coelho

Simple Wealth Inevitable Wealth
By Nick Murray

Acknowledgments

I would like to thank and acknowledge many folks for everything they have done to help me out with this book and in life.

First, I would like to thank my wife, Erin, the love of my life, who puts up with me on a daily, sometimes hourly basis. I am appreciative of all the conversations, edits, ideas, and so on that were exchanged between the two of us about the book. Also, time was taken from our marriage (time opportunity cost) to complete this goal for the benefit of others! I love you! I am proud of you and your successes as a business owner, mom, and photographer.

Thank you to my daughter, the newest love of my life, who has already taught me to be a better person in 2 1/2 short years. I hope someday you and your family may benefit greatly from the multiple streams of income Daddy plans to establish. I love how you keep Mama and me on our toes constantly. You already show signs of determination and persistence. Please, do not ever let those disappear, but only temper them when needed. Thanks for understanding that I needed to take countless hours out from being "Daddy" and work on these words to make our world a better place.

Thanks to my parents, Joe and Julie Romas, for making the sacrifices I know about and those of which I have no knowledge. The opportunities for Stefanie and myself were second to none. Now that I am a parent, I am much more aware of how wonderful I had it and how hard you worked to make me who I am today. I love you. Thank you both.

Thank you to my sister, Stefanie (Romas) Herbert, for helping out with first round edits. Very kind of you to donate your time to "help a brother out."

Thank you to Stephanie McBride for a wonderfully laid-out and distinctive cover.

Thank you to Kira Henschel of HenschelHaus Publishing from Milwaukee, Wisconsin. Without you, I would not have been able to begin manifesting the ideas I had burning inside my head. Also, thank you for helping me with some illustrations that were messy and hand-drawn. I never claim to have received an A in art class. At least not that I can recall.

Thank you to Jay Papason, co-author of *The One Thing*. I appreciate your insights and input into the world writing, publishing, and marketing.

I'd like to thank Dave Ramsey, Phil Demuth, Ph.D., Bill Madsen, Jim Asplin, Greg Buboltz, Bruce Waller, Joe Torelli, Matt Clinton, Don Rude, Deborah Oelke, Terry Pruett, Amber Scarborough from Scarborough Financial, Cash Matthews from The Solomon Group, Bill Simonet from Simonet Wealth Management, and the College for Financial Planning® for their mentorship and imparting their wisdom on a fellow advisor. Except for some of my own analogies, this book is a compilation of the knowledge these books and individuals have poured into me. Any and all errors in this book are strictly my own and can be attributed only to myself.

BIBLIOGRAPHY

College for Financial Planning. *Asset Allocation & Selection.* 2012

DeMuth, Phil. *The Affluent Investor: Financial Advice to Grow and Protect Your Wealth.* Hauppauge, NY: Barron's Educational Series, Inc. 2013

Gladwell, Malcolm. *Outliers: The Story of Success.* Little, Brown, 2008

Kahneman, Daniel and Tversky, Amos. "Prospect Theory: An Analysis of Decision Under Risk." *Econometrica.* Vol. 47, No. 2 (March 1979), pp. 263-292

The Lampo Group, Inc. *Financial Peace University.* Brentwood, TN, 1994

Murray, Nick. *Behavioral Investment Counseling.* The Nick Murray Company, Inc. 2008

Siegel, Jeremy J. *Stocks for the Long Run.* McGraw-Hill, 1994

About the Author

Joe Romas was born and raised in Milwaukee, Wisconsin. He is a former Student Naval Aviator, Naval Officer (Lieutentant), as well as a former high school math and special education teacher. He began his career with a large financial services company and decided to become an independent financial advisor to benefit his clients and prospective clients. Joe decided since he is an entrepreneur at heart, to make the entrepreneurial "leap of faith" and begin Romas Wealth Management. Already, it has paid off tremendously.

In his spare time, he enjoys golfing, reading, watching and cheering for the Green Bay Packers, bicycling, playing with Sofia (his daughter), wine and (light) beer tasting, loose-leaf tea sampling, spending time with his wife Erin, and helping her with her successful photography business Vintage Peach Photography, www.vintagepeachphoto.com.

For more information visit:
http://www.joeromas.com

Connect with me on Facebook and Linked In

CPSIA information can be obtained at www.ICGtesting.com
Printed in the USA
LVOW05s2158230715

447468LV00036B/427/P